Abstract

Recent technological innovation initiatives have tended to place too much emphasis on the importance of knowledge creation with acceleration of technological development and adaptation and greater market competition, innovation is a prerequisite for enterprise survival. Innovation activity encompasses industry, business houses and government institutions. The Wenzhou model has been restructured and scaled up through four strategic choices: institutional change, technological upgrading, industrial diversification, and spatial restructuring (Wei, 2009; Wei, Li & Wang, 2007). The study addresses innovation and regional development, sharing findings that promote innovation, thus enhancing economic, technological and regional development through new economic activities that stimulate wealth, employment and growth generation and increase competitiveness. Although Perroux set his poles in the abstract notion of economic space, regional development theories, such as Friedmann(1966,1972), applied these theories directly to physical space with the concept of growth poles. Research on China has unfolded the substantial regional inequality and multiple pathways of regional development (Wei, 2007). Developing countries are increasingly driving the performance of the world economy. Trade between developing countries is becoming as important as trade between them and developed economies. Through a comprehensive review of the literature on globalization, industrial restructuring and regional development. This paper holds that the research on Rondonia is embedded in Brazil's reform process, as well as theoretical development in economic geography. It highlights the important role of institutions and global -local interactions in industrial and regional development. The intra-industry has a positive impact on economic growth (Grubel and Lloyd, 1975). This paper confirms relevant theoretical hypothesis as foreign direct investment and globalization promotes the economic growth. The good results obtained with GMM system estimator suggest that the building of dynamic theoretical models will be of interest to academic researchers. Rondonia is a state of opportunities and euphoria. The study directly linked to economic development such as industrialization and adding technology to the primary production. The key issues research deals with the question of land regularization in the state of Rondonia which is directly linked to development, particularly in terms of access to credit. The key challenges for the above study deals with defending the environmental concerns and also to ensure the right social balance in the population. This means the recuperation of powers to be able to include the 25% of the Rondonia population living in poverty. The above project will be eye opening for the entrepreneurs, traders, producers, small scale producers and investors by increasing access to use technology in production in order to be able to export products with added values for Rondonia/Brazil as imports and export grew in 2013 by 62%. O'Neill, global economist at Goldman Sachs, suggests the economic potential of Brazil, Russia, India, and China is such that they may become among the four most dominant economies by the year 2050.The instruments of regional development promotion broadly divided into three categories: tax and financial incentives; long term and short term credit and public investment, both of the government properly said, and of the state enterprises. The study discusses the public strategy initiatives for formulating projects to Western Amazon area, highlighting the projects of hydro power plant complex, and water way construction along the way of Madeira River at Rondônia state, where the natural resources utilization tends to make potent to improve the population social conditions through the energy offer, stimulates new enterprises and employment opportunities. The industry sector has been growing a lot. Rondônia is a state that is highly agricultural, with more than 20 meat processing plants within, the state, and soya bean production has been growing a lot. In 2012, recorded export of 1.6 billion, where the 3 main items on the roaster were: boneless meat, soya bean and Cassiterite. Rondonia's GDP is growing at

Chinese rates, especially because of the investments in the electrical sector. Rondônia is the only state of the Northern region of in Brazil where the GDP of the interior is greater than the GDP of the capital. Rondônia had a population of 36,935 people in 1950, the population increased to 888,430 in 1980. But most migrants did not get any land upon the arrival in Rondônia and the local indigenous population often lost the land that they already possessed. The state of Rondônia appears to be part of the land policy of the Brazilian state, by the increasing expansion of big landlords, by the destruction of Amazon forest. This expansion of landlord's front is the major cause of the agrarian conflicts. So the study raises the key issues on the exclusion from landownership for Rondônia population creating unemployment and poverty. Guajará-Mirim, situated in the state of Rondônia, and borders the city of Guayara-Mirim in Bolivia. It covers an area of 82.5 square kilometers, including the urban perimeter of Guajará-Mirim, in northeastern Rondônia. The regional economic is concentrated on agriculture, mining and large hydroelectric enterprises (UHE). Mining activities in Brazil not only generate important streams of revenue for federal and local governments but also directly and indirectly contribute to the local economies and provide training and employment for a large number of people. The study would focuses on improving infrastructure, lowering taxes and training workers for the industry using the latest technology in the market for mining. The study focuses on the key issues of skilled labor force and logistics to reduce tax burdens, to be able to improve the environment of generating business, and also the environment of providing incentive to the business sector in regards to production, competitions and market insertion international.

Keywords: Globalization, Industrialization, Technological development, Regional development.

1. Introduction

Recent technological innovation initiatives have tended to place too much emphasis on the importance of knowledge creation with acceleration of technological development and adaptation and greater market competition, innovation is a prerequisite for enterprise survival. Innovation activity encompasses industry, business houses and government institutions. The Wenzhou model has been restructured and scaled up through four strategic choices: institutional change, technological upgrading, industrial diversification, and spatial restructuring (Wei, 2009; Wei, Li & Wang, 2007). The study addresses innovation and regional development, sharing findings that promote innovation, thus enhancing economic, technological and regional development through new economic activities that stimulate wealth, employment and growth generation and increase competitiveness. Innovation must be harnessed to tackle global problems effectively and efficiently.

Innovation in green technologies, for example, can help us fight climate change without sacrificing growth. But getting solutions to market will require the right incentives to spur innovation and development. Fortunately, there is evidence that innovation in climate change mitigation technologies is accelerating. Innovation can also help us speed up social improvements in developing countries. It's a powerful tool for combating infectious diseases and producing clean drinking water, for example. The ability to address these increasingly urgent issues depends on stronger innovation and new forms of international collaboration.

Different global challenges naturally call for different approaches; nevertheless, some common strategies are emerging to accelerate scientific progress and diffuse innovation as widely as possible: we need greater involvement of the private sector, nongovernmental and philanthropic organizations; we need to build greater capacity for innovation in developing countries, including through technology transfer; and, to do these, we need to devise new financing mechanisms. Although Perroux set his poles in the abstract notion of economic space, regional development theories, such as Friedmann (1966, 1972), applied these theories directly to physical space with the concept of growth poles. Research on China has unfolded the substantial regional inequality and multiple pathways of regional development (Wei, 2007).

Developing countries are increasingly driving the performance of the world economy. Innovation and technological change are central to the quest for regional development. In the globally-connected knowledge-driven economy, the relevance of agglomeration forces that rely on proximity continues to increase, paradoxically despite declining real costs of information, communication and transportation. Globally, the proportion of the population living in cities continues to grow and sprawling cities remain the engines of regional economic transformation.

The growth of cities results from a complex chain that starts with scale, density and geography, which then combines with industrial structure characterized by its extent of specialization, competition and diversity, to yield innovation and productivity growth that encourages employment expansion, and further urban growth through inward migration trade between developing countries is becoming as important as trade between them and developed economies. Through a comprehensive review of the literature on globalization, industrial restructuring and regional development. This paper holds that the research on Rondônia is embedded in Brazil's reform process, as well as theoretical development in economic geography. It highlights the important role of institutions and global –local interactions in industrial and regional development. The intra-industry has a positive impact on economic growth (Grubel and Lloyd, 1975).

The study focuses on the main objectives and strategies are as follows:

Reduction of regional inequalities: Equity is the key word here. That principle will translate into a tireless fight for reducing the inequalities of income among regions, for opening up new economic opportunities for lagged regions, and for improving the working conditions all over the country.

Efficiency and Competitiveness: Designing mechanisms to orient public and private investment decisions toward reaching higher levels of efficiency and competitiveness (especially) in less developed regions is to be another fundamental principle of the new regional policy.

Territorial fragmentation: For the new government, large economies such as ours are in need of policies capable of combining the internal integrative effort with a progressive opening to the world market. While some regions are already relatively open to external trade, a deliberate effort is in order to avoid that certain areas be kept at the margin, more and more condemned to a state of permanent poverty.

Concentration of production: The government will stimulate a reduction of regional concentration of productive assets and of production, by strengthening local specializations. The new regional policy will deal differently with the various kinds of regions. A proposed classification is as following: (1) Dynamic Areas (i.e. areas that are doing well, and whose productive capacity is modern and competitive); (2) Areas Under Restructuring (i. e. areas which used to be rich and competitive; have been changing their economic structure; but still are potentially competitive); (3) Stagnated Areas (areas of low economic dynamism); (4) Undeveloped Areas (i.e. areas that have been kept aside of the economic development process, and whose potential has to be better known and explored);(5) Borderline Areas (i.e. areas near the country's Western and Northern borders, that present specific problems and need special attention of the federal government).

The National Council of Regional Policy: The new government will propose the creation of a National Council of Regional Policy, and of a National Fund of Regional Development, the latter conceived of as an instrument that will enable the government to reach the objective of reducing regional inequalities. It will be a statutory responsibility of the Council to analyze the regional impacts of sector policies. The new regional policy will be partly financed by the National Fund, whose administration will be democratized.

2. Research Methodology:

This paper confirms relevant theoretical hypothesis as foreign direct investment and globalization promotes the economic growth. The good results obtained with GMM system estimator suggest that the building of dynamic theoretical models will be of interest to academic researchers. Rondônia is a state of opportunities and euphoria. The study directly linked to economic development such as industrialization and adding technology to the primary production. The key issues research deals with the question of land regularization in the state of

Rondônia which is directly linked to development, particularly in terms of access to credit. The key challenges for the above study deals with defending the environmental concerns and also to ensure the right social balance in the population.

This means the recuperation of powers to be able to include the 25% of the Rondônia population living in poverty. The above project will be eye opening for the entrepreneurs, traders, producers, small scale producers and investors by increasing access to use technology in production in order to be able to export products with added values for Rondônia as imports and export grew in 2013 by 62%.In terms of infrastructure, the main project we are working on is the construction and installation of a new public port and within this port structure we are going to install an Export Processing Zone. We are also looking for investors and investment to increase our export possibilities. We are opening a new area for limestone exploration.

Our government has always had and still has strong concerns about the environment and so this limestone production area is going to allow us to improve and maximize production without deforestation and actually recuperating some areas and stimulating small and medium producers. The port is essential for us to be able to increase our capabilities and to bring in private investment. We have seen growing demand in the Asian market for our commodities, but we must add technology to benefit these products particularly soy, maize, rice, minerals and wood. To be able to have private investment we need to have cheaper alternatives for production distribution. We don't have a lot of consumer markets close to us for our industrial production. Our population is just one to one and a half million, we have Mato Grosso do Sul next to us and Amazonia which have low population densities, and therefore we need infrastructure: roads, highways and ports. The port is essential. The current port is 60,000 m2, the new public port will be 1 million m2 and with the possibility of expansion. Within the public port we will have 259 hectares for the Export Processing Zone which is approximately 2 million 600 thousand square meters.

So the EPZ is a new project and a new centre for the country's industrialization process and Rondônia, particularly the city of Porto Velho was chosen for this. In this zone, industries will set up and benefit from a series of distribution incentives from the unions and the state to export this production. 20% of our production goes to the internal market and pays taxes like any other company; however the production that is exported will not pay these taxes. Therefore through this port and the Madeira River, with the dredging that has been planned by the federal government we can export this production. Even in the dry season we can get to the Atlantic and reach markets not only in the north east but also in other countries. We also have links to the Pacific through Peru and Bolivia. This trans-pacific highway is nearly finished and will enable us to reach the Asian markets without passing through the Panama Canal, reducing time and costs as the canal is very expensive to use.

Jim O'Neill, global economist at Goldman Sachs, suggests the economic potential of Brazil, Russia, India, and China is such that they may become among the four most dominant economies by the year 2050.The instruments of regional development promotion broadly divided into three categories: tax and financial incentives; long term and short term credit and public investment, both of the government properly said, and of the state enterprises. The study discusses the public strategy initiatives for formulating projects to Western Amazon area, highlighting the projects of hydro power plant complex, and water way construction along the way of Madeira River at Rondonia state, where the natural resources utilization tends to make potent to improve the population social conditions through the energy offer, stimulates new enterprises and employment opportunities.

The industry sector has been growing a lot. Rondonia is a state that is highly agricultural, with more than 20 meat processing plants within, the state, and soyabean production has been growing a lot. In 2012, recorded export of 1.6 billion, where the 3 main items on the roaster were: boneless meat, soyabean and

Cassiterite.Rondonia's GDP is growing at Chinese rates, especially because of the investments in the electrical sector. Rondonia is the only state of the Northern region of Brazil where the GDP of the interior is greater than the GDP of the capital. Rondonia had a population of 36,935 people in 1950, the population increased to 888,430 in 1980. But most migrants did not get any land upon the arrival in Rondonia and the local indigenous population often lost the land that they already possessed. The state of Rondonia appears to be part of the land policy of the Brazilian state, by the increasing expansion of big landlords, by the destruction of Amazon forest.

This expansion of landlords front is the major cause of the agrarian conflicts. So the study raises the key issues on the exclusion from landownership for Rondonia population creating unemployment and poverty. Guajará-Mirim, situated in the state of Rondônia, and borders the city of Guayaramirim in Bolivia. It covers an area of 82.5 square kilometers, including the urban perimeter of Guajará-Mirim, in northeastern Rondônia. The regional economic is concentrated on agriculture, mining and livestock. Mining activities in Brazil not only generate important streams of revenue for federal and local governments but also directly and indirectly contribute to the local economies and provide training and employment for a large number of people.The study would focuses on improving infrastructure, lowering taxes and training workers for the industry using the latest technology in the market for mining ornamental rocks.

3. General Aspects

It presents general aspects of globalization and mining in Rondônia, Brazil.

3.1 Globalization

The implications of globalization for a national economy are many. Globalization has intensified interdependence and competition between economies in the world market. This is reflected in Interdependence in regard to trading in goods and services and in movement of capital. As a result domestic economic developments are not determined entirely by domestic policies and market conditions. Rather, they are influenced by both domestic and international policies and economic conditions. It is thus clear that a globalizing economy, while formulating and evaluating its domestic policy cannot afford to ignore the possible actions and reactions of policies and developments in the rest of the world. This constrained the policy option available to the government which implies loss of policy autonomy to some extent, in decision-making at the national level. The results for international trade in value added of the Brazilian states – aggregated by all source / destination industries and countries, so that we can focus attention on the states – are presented in Table 1.

Table 1: International trade in Value Added, Rondonia,2008- Million US$

	Exports	% value added	Import	% value added	Surplus	% value added
Rondonia	634	7.4%	773	9.0%	-139	-1.6%

Sources: http://www.usp.br/nereus/wp-content/uploads/TD_Nereus_13_2013.pdf

We have observed that Rondonia trade in value added is somewhat limited. So, it is interesting to more carefully analyze the trade of Rondonia. Do they trade? And, if yes, with whom? Table 2 aims to add to this question, showing the composition of trade in value added of the Rondonia, as in 2008. For example, according to Table 2, in 2008, 68% of Rondonia's value added was generated for its own final use (domestic share), 25.1% for rest of Rondonia's final use (regional exports' share. Moreover, Rondonia's final use led to purchases in value added from other Brazilian states amounted in 42.4% of its own total value added (regional imports' share). As a result, Rondonia's regional trade presented a negative surplus corresponding to -17% of its value added.

Table 2. Domestic and Regional Shares in Total Trade in Value Added, Rondonia, 2008

	Domestic	Regional exports	Regional Imports	Regional surplus	Internatio-nal surplus
Rondonia	68%	25.1%	42.4%	-17%	-2%

Sources: http://www.usp.br/nereus/wp-content/uploads/TD_Nereus_13_2013.pdf

3.2 Mining in Rondônia:

The study focuses on the key issues of skilled labour force and logistics to reduce tax burdens, able to improve the environment of generating business, and also the environment of providing incentive to the business sector in regards to production and competitions. The country's mining sector is going through a phase of real euphoria following the minerals boom, which has led o an increase in net foreign direct investment. The stability of the national economy, as shown by the successive drops in the sovereign-risk index, and the country's competitive position in the world market, has attracted investors and boosted their confidence in the country. The mining industry in Rondônia also promises a great investment opportunity for foreign investors.

The state is one of the leading producers of tin. The state alone accounts for 25% of the country's tin production. The state of Rondônia has a good granite industry. Granite constitutes about 8.7% of the state's exports. The granite produced in Rondonia has a very peculiar characteristic – it has an illuminated background with brown spots on it. Foreign investors can also consider investing in the granite industry of Rondonia. The mining industry in Rondonia also promises great investment opportunity foreign investors. The state is one of the leading producers of Tin. The state alone accounts for 25% of the country's Tin production. The state of Rondonia has a good granite industry. Granite constitutes about 8.7% of the state's exports. The study will be eye opening for the foreign investors to invest in the granite industry of Rondonia.

During the past decades, the mining industry has effectively contributed to the improvement of the living standards of population, generating new jobs and building infrastructures for the region. The contribution of the mining sector to the sustainable development of that region is relevant and effective. The study focuses on the major threats to eco- systems for the mining. Mineral processing and extractive metallurgy are devoted to the scientific, engineering, and economic aspects of the extraction, preparation, separation, and purification of ores, metals, and mineral products by physical, chemical, pyro metallurgical, hydro metallurgical, magnetic and biological (e.g. microbes) methods.

4. Bangalore, India – A Case Study of Globalization, ICT and Regional Development

An excellent example of linkage of global and local network can be seen in Bangalore, a mega-city in India. In the midst of software network firms with more than 100 multinational firms and many other large, medium and small firms there exists a network of activities of slum dwellers with the objective of bringing them into a global system alleviating poverty and destitution. However, it is a very difficult task and it is unlikely that the effort will succeed. Another significant aspect of the experience of Bangalore is the attempted cooperation of federal, state and local government institutions, educational institutions and the private sector. Bangalore is the capitol of the state of Karnataka which is the eighth largest in India in terms of population and area. Both the state government and the federal government have included (with the cooperation of the private sector) an ambitious plan to develop the airport, power, roads, water supply, etc. However, the work is going very slowly and the situation has come to a stage where the growth in Bangalore may slow down and move to other competing areas like Hyderabad, Mumbai in Delhi. The plan of establishing software technology parks (STPs) starting in 1988 with 100% allowable foreign equity, no taxes on imports hardware and software, high speed data communication, security, independent telephone facilities, uninterrupted power supply, etc. was a motivating factor for the growth in Bangalore. There is also private sector cooperative organizations like Bangalore Action Task Force (BATF) that are helping to improve the infrastructure of the city. Thus, Bangalore is providing an excellent example of how globalization and localization are acting together.

The revitalization in Bangalore, making it India's Silicon Valley, was engineered by transnational corporations. However, existence of low wage skilled labor is not the only reason TNC came to Bangalore. There are other sectors in India like pharmaceuticals where the same situation exists. But there has not been a dramatic movement in that sector. It is because of the non-existence of an innovative system in pharmaceuticals. Economic reforms, previous policy of import substitutions, market boom in software demand worldwide, devaluation of currency and low wage technical workers drew the transnational corporations. Although the firms could prosper with a low wage rate but also low productivity relative to its potential, scarcity of labor resources leading to higher wages eventually led to technological progress and economic efficiency. If this trend does not persist, the industry will move to other Indian regions and foreign countries.

In Bangalore, side-by-side with the multinational and big Indian companion, there exists large members of small and medium size units with 10-50 employees (local assemblers still dominate

50% of PC market). In many ways, the nature of innovation processes in these small enterprises is similar to those in U.K. and Scandinavian countries and other western countries. Unlike other Indian regions in India, the factors such as existence of universities and research facilities to develop skilled workers and new technologies, existence of multinationals, entrepreneurial drive, availability of venture capital, etc. are mainly responsible. New product development through radical innovation (Cooke, 2001) by these small enterprises came primarily through self-motivation and the perception of new opportunities. Improvement of existing product through incremental innovation resulted due to customer pressure. The former effort is directed towards growth and export whereas the latter is just to stay in the market. Incremental innovation took place due to external factors and for radical innovation it is internal. Whereas the support for technology development from governments in India for small units is mostly through technology transfer, in Western countries it is through funding research projects and research grants. This low intensity on R&D of all industries particularly small industries, lack of technical background of entrepreneurs gives India a low technical achievement index (TAI).

The informational and network society in Bangalore and its role of the development of socio-political development of the urban landscape is, in many ways, similar to the Silicon Valleys of other developing countries but in sharp contrast of the developed world. It is reinforcing the unjust socio-political divisions, defranchising the poor and developing information-age-elites. This is in tune with Castell's (1996) transformation theory of globalization, informational mode of transportation and urban regional transplantation. Its theoretical basis can be seen in Paul Krugman's (Chatterji and Gangopadhyay, 2005) theory of center and periphery. The basic approach of Castell of restructuring of capitalism (global shift of capital, weak labor, state support for high-tech industries away from welfare activities) is the change in the development informational mode (use of computers) and more decentralization, separation of knowledge (elites vs. manual workers) and urban regional transformation leading to high demand for knowledge workers. (Madon and Sahay, 2001)

Developing technology (radical or incremental) is not enough. It is the role of the entrepreneur (Sunder, 2004) to bring it to the market. In India this process is yet to start and needs to be nurtured. The process of globalization has greatly accentuated the role of entrepreneur. India has a long history of providing this spirit. But what is needed is more encouragement and removing the obstacles. The government's policy should not be to protect and encourage public sector enterprise but also help private sector particularly small scale innovators and encourage venture capitalists. There is also a bias towards foreign and large corporations in procurement orders. Corporate procurement processes work against the small vendor.

The government can play (Van Dijk, 2003) a significant role in further developing the technology cluster in Bangalore. It can provide appropriate industrial policy, education and training, market support, physical infrastructure, opening research centers and incubators. At the time of world-wide recession, it should also be prepared to act as a cushion. The importance of social embeddedness (Parthasarathy, 2006) of economic activity – tying state and local capital to bring economic transformation has been discussed widely in the literature. When the state was autonomous and there was limited embeddedness, like in India before the mid-80s, it hindered the ability of states in India to take global opportunities. After that period things changed. However, although the state was not in the way, it was not helpful enough. Although embeddedness is a necessary condition it is not sufficient. There has to be a balance between the two as we have seen in newly industrialized countries (NIC).

A significant change is taking place in the Bangalore cluster. It is moving from the position of low-wage, low-skilled software providers to high-skill R&D services. (Parthasarathy, 2006) It is moving up the global supply chain specializing in design and value-added R&D services. Although the state was a major player with multinational companies, this product and intersectional upgrading is taking place with the help of local entrepreneurs. Indians returning home helped. Institutional thickness (previously missing) and a high level of interaction are fast developing. The type of R&D services they are pursuing is a combination of hardware and software to perform a specific task without human interaction like voice-data convergence since the distinction between hardware and software designs are vanishing. In this area one can be a chip vendor (requiring substantial investment), design services provider or seller of intellectual property (IP) blocks. There are some companies designing semiconductor chips and applying for patents. In the beginning, Bangalore started with major service provider. Another entrepreneurial group providing R&D and local networks among local firms is emerging. The multinational corporations are taking advantage of local expertise rather than providing it as they did before. Absence of local manufacturing facilities poses no problem since many of the Indian firms have oversees collaboration particularly in NIC. The technological upgrading led by multinational corporations is being replaced by local expertise. Informal networks have also increased tremendously. Whether what is happening now in upgrading in

Bangalore can be repeated someplace else (Hyderabad) or it will be sustainable is something to be seen.

There has been considerable work on the efficiency (Caniels and Romijn, 2003) of industrial clusters and spatial proximity, under the heading of the Collective Efficiency (CE) approach. In an agglomeration the enterprises are doing similar activities pursued by several units in a cluster which brings local external economies including economies of scale, scope and transaction automatically for which a particular unit does not have to make any efforts to attain it. On the other hand, there are some advantages like exchange of information and knowledge spillover where the unit has to actively seek. However, the benefit for getting this information far outweighs its costs. Thus (Caniels and Romijn, 2003), there can be four basic types of agglomeration advantages: (1) spontaneous cost advantages, (2) spontaneous spillover, (3) facilitated cost advantages and (4) facilitated spillover. The examples in (1) are economies of scale, critical local minimum demand and local presence of specialized supplies. The examples for (2) are demonstration effects, human capital formations and inter-firm movement of trained labor. For (3) examples are teaming up for joint project and reducing risk in addition to advantages in (2) except that effort is needed on the part of the enterprises. In addition of intra-firms and inter-firms forces, the advantages can accrue due to international technology transfer, governmental policy with respect to infrastructure development and regulation.

Caniels and Romijn uses the empirical materials available from different sources for Bangalore to explain their framework of efficiency and capability building.

Macroeconomic policies of the central, state and local governments, international technology industries development, outsourcing, etc. greatly influenced Bangalore growth. We have discussed these factors before.

Dynamic changes were already taking place in the information technology sector of Bangalore. They have already begun to obtain ISO certification and have moved from low skill, low wage export oriented software development to research and development leading to upgraded products. Many of the companies are devoting considerable amounts of resources to training and development. It is not just the multinational companies but small and large Indian companies are impacting the training leading to capacity building. (Parthasarathy, 2004, 2006) The link of the clusters to the U.S. software sector particularly through human capital and increase in foreign direct investment and economic reform greatly accelerated the growth of Bangalore clusters. It is difficult to say at this stage how accumulated firm level capabilities can influence to increase agglomeration economics further. Existence of many small scale enterprises, specialized suppliers, inter-firm movement of labor, well established forum of information exchange, returned emigrants provided spontaneous knowledge spillover.

Although there is increased joint private and public sector effort in improving the infrastructure as a response to growth, there is no evidence that agglomeration advantages due to deliberate effort on the part of the enterprises are forthcoming. It appears that the multinational corporations (Patibandla and Petersoen, 2003) are reluctant to reveal the "higher-end" knowledge and the possibility is only for horizontal cooperation of Indian large enterprises of the same size. Due to the huge labor turnover small and medium size enterprises are reluctant to share knowledge but there are some interactions in different levels of the value chain. In the case of Bangalore "old economy" (Marsallian factors) play an overriding role compared to "new economy" factors. In this way, agglomeration economies of knowledge based industries differ between developed and developing countries. (D'Costa 2006, Audirac 2003, Bala Subrahmanya 2005)

It is often stated that the Bangalore cluster is exceedingly dependent on export-oriented low wage, low skill activities susceptible to cyclical trends. Particularly the interaction between industry, academia and government is missing in spite of a long history of development in technical education in

Bangalore, economic reform and change of attitudes of the governments, etc. (D'Costa, 2006) There is a serious shortage of Ph.D level engineers who can devote their energy to research and development. The educational system at the post-graduate level and the high school level are particularly to blame. There is lack of trust amongst the enterprises due to excessive competition. What is needed is vigorous cooperation between educational and research institutions, business and government in the scale which is happening in the biotechnology field.

The growth of a cluster depends on other things like quality of life, composition of the economic and economic class of the community, provision of infrastructure and human capital. (Wu, 2005) The questions to ask are: "What types of cities are creative? What location factors are essential? What are the urban policy initiatives used by creative cities?" Agglomeration economies are not generated purely on intra- and inter-firm linkages but also on overall external factors. A crucial factor is the political economy. For example, in the state of Andhra Pradesh where Cybercity Hyderabad (competitor of Bangalore) is located, voters in state elections overwhelmingly rejected the further growth of the IT cluster and the state is reverted back to develop the village economy.

There is a need to research the agglomeration economies of knowledge industries in Bangalore using more sophisticated analytical tools of Regional Science. We hope this will be done in the near future.

5. Final Considerations

The recent economic boom in the fast developing countries (China and India being such examples) has resulted in a sharp increase in the demand for minerals and metals. As the world's more viable deposits deplete, there will be an acute need to develop deposits currently considered sub-economic. The processing of such deposits may be more energy intensive due to the application of deep-level mining techniques. As a consequence, the energy requirements of the mining industries are expected to increase exponentially with an attendant increase in the generation of mine-related waste.

To sustain consistent competitive levels requires the development of processing technologies that:

1.   Require less energy,

2.   Consume less water,

3.   Require lower capital cost,

4.   Produce lower dust levels, gas emissions, and less toxic effluent, and

5.   Produce higher value-added graduation of final products.

The search for new and innovative mining technologies that would increase productivity, improve health and safety and maintain competitiveness has been relentless since the early nineties. The recent growing awareness of the adverse environmental and ecological impacts of mining has provided an additional driver.

Increasing Depths of Mining: As mining progresses to greater depths, increases in rock stress require innovative designs to ensure the short-term and long-term stability of the mine structure.

Continuous Mining: Truly continuous mining will require an accelerated search for innovative fragmentation and material handling systems.

Real-Time Information Systems: Techniques for sensing, analysis, and communication and information management have become increasingly important. Each mining environment presents unique challenges to the design and operation of equipment. Increasing the productive operating time of equipment and mining systems will require modern monitoring technologies.

The entire mining process would benefit from technology advancement in many sectors. However, focus should be primarily in four key areas:

(1) Rock fragmentation with the goal of achieving continuous mining and conserving overall energy consumption;

(2) Sensors and sensor systems for mechanical, chemical, and hydrological applications;

(3) Data processing and visualization methods that produce real-time feedback; and

(4) Automation and control systems.

The industries in the ceramics sector in general are seeing continued investment. Today in the state of Rondônia there are 10 ceramics factories with the largest and best kilns. So the study depicts to modernize the sector with innovative technological machines and equipments in increasing the production rate and to achieve the best quality.

6. References:

Bala Subrahmanya, M.H. "Pattern of technological innovations in small enterprises: a comparative perspective of Bangalore (India) and Northeast England (UK)." *Technovation*, 2005: pp. 269-280.

Caniels and Romijn. "Dynamic Clusters in Developing Countries: Collective Efficiency and Beyond." *Oxford Development Studies*. Volume 31 (2003): pp. 275-292.

Castells, M. *The Rise of the Network Societ.* Oxford: Blackwell, 1996.

Chang, H.-J. (2003c). Globalization, economic development and the role of the state (London and New York: Zed Books; Penang, Malaysia: Third World Network).

Chatterji and Gangopadhyay. *Economic Globalization in Asia.* Aldershot: Ashgate, 2005

Cooke, Philip. "New Economy Innovation Systems: Biotechnology in Europe and the USA." *Industry and Innovation.* Volume 8 (2001): pp. 267-289.

D'Costa, Anthony P. "Exports, University-Industry Linkages, and Innovation Challenges in Bangalore, India." *World Bank Policy Research Working Paper*, 2006.

Dietzenbacher, Erik,. Guilhoto, Joaquim J.M and Imori, Denise. 2013. The role of Brazilian regions in the global value.

Friedmann, J.1996. Regional Development Policy: A Case Study of Venezuela. Cambridge: MIT Press.

Friedmann,J.1972. A general Theory of Polarized Development in Growth Centers in Regional Economic Development.ed. N.M.Hansen.82-107. New York. Free Press.

Grubel, H. and Lloyd, P.(1975). "Intra-industry trade: the theory and measurement of international trade in different products", London: Macmillan.

Lin, G.C.S., & Wang, C.(2009). Technological innovation in China's high-tech sector. Eurasian Geography and Economics, 50(4), 402-424.

Parthasarathy, Balaji. "India's Silicon Valley or Silicon Valley's India? Socially Embedding the Computer Software Industry in Bangalore." *International Journal of Urban and Regional Research*. Volume 28.3 (2004): pp. 664-85.

Patibandla and Petersen. "Role of Transitional Corporations in the Evolution of a High-Tech Industry: The Case of India's Software Industry-A Reply." *World Development*. Volume 32 (2004): pp. 561-566.

Wei, Y.H.D.,Zhou, Y., Sun, Y.F., & Lin, G.C.S (2012). Production and R&D networks of foreign ventures in China:

Implications for technological dynamism and regional development. Applied Geography, 32(1), 106-118.

Wei, Y.H.D(2007). Regional development in China:transitional institutions, embedded globalization and hybrid economics. Eurasian Geography and Economics, 48(1), 16-36.

Wei, Y.H.D (2009). China's Shoe manuafacturing and the Wenzhou model. Eurasian Geography and Economics, 50(6), 720-739.

Wei, Y.H.D.(2007). Regional development in China: transitional institutions, embedded globalization and hybrid economies. Eurasian Geography and Economics, 48(1), 16-36.

Wei, Y.H.D.,Li,W.M., & Wang.C.B.(2007). Restructuring industrial districts scaling up regional development: a study of the Wenzhou model, China. Economic Geography, 83(4), 421-444.

Wu, Weiping. "Dynamic Cities and Creative Clusters." World Bank Policy Research Working Paper, 2005.

Van Dijk, Meine Pieter. "Government Policies with respect to an

Information Technology Cluster in Bangalore, India." *The European Journal of Development Research.* Volume 15 (2003): pp. 93-108.

www.ingramcontent.com/pod-product-compliance
Lightning Source LLC
Chambersburg PA
CBHW051827170526
45167CB00005B/2183